Forward

There comes a time of awakening in everyone. For some it is ignored because it is not "normal" thought. Others realize this awakening and change direction in life. Now is the time for you to wake up and recognize the lies and deception that have chained you down by others.

It's not that they have done it on purpose. Years of indoctrination by parents and teachers that have become sheep by the machine that is corporate America have turned their will to mush. Go to college, get a degree, find a trade, get a job will accomplish survival at best. Think about it! Is survival what you really want? Where in the human mind does this make sense? Take most people that have a job in America for example. The average shmuck walks around with just enough money to cover lunch in their pocket and a couple of just about full credit cards in their pocket! Time for a reality check, is this you?

Here is the truth. Corporate America per capita makes very few millionaires per capita than the lifestyle I am about to advocate. To get you thinking on a different plane you'll find that this book has no chapters or page numbers and no fluff. To break the chains first we have to break the mold. It's the truth and it will set you free……….

See you almost missed the first page! Books are laid out in a certain style or arrangement. Who says it needs to be that way? If I can write this any way I want, then you can manage your career and wealth the way you want. Let's free your mind.

Too many Americans wake up every day to an alarm clock, roll out of bed, take their anxiety meds and roll into work. They sit in a cubicle, or behind some sort of machine for eight hours and head home in a vehicle they really would rather they didn't own in rush hour traffic. They park in the street or in a driveway of a home they struggle to keep and are met by a spouse with a pile of bills and a dinner they would rather not have. Why is this? From the outside looking in is this something you "always wanted"? To me, it sucks! I know because I did it! Hmmm! Has you thinking doesn't it?

The fact is you are better off under your own care than with what someone else decides you can have or is what's best for you.

Check this out! I just single spaced between paragraphs because I can! Corporate America would never let you do this. Some suit would change your memo or their secretary Mrs. Hammertoes would have surely caught this terrible and career limiting blunder. Why? What does it change? Nothing, absolutely nothing. It makes no difference monetarily or in the information in the book. Again, stereotypes are holding you back!

When you were in school, did you ever wonder why you were taught English, Math and Science? Did anybody ever tell you that you needed it for your own benefit? Indeed some of us were.

Did you remember everyone telling each other what they wanted to be? Police man, Fireman,

Astronaut, all admirable professions. But, who dreamed about working in a cubicle? What about an office the size of a broom closet with no windows? How about the kid that wanted to work for a company into their fifties when their job would be suddenly outsourced? Welcome to Corporate America!

Ha, ha, you say! I'm in a trade union! That's not me! Sorry to tell you this, but all of that money you were promised would be in your retirement account? Guess what? It won't be there! Just ask the guys that are retiring now!

I really don't think that either Unions or Corporate America are evil because they aren't. The fact, which is contrary to popular belief is that Corporate America has less to offer and slimmer chances for success than many other opportunities.

The real fact is that corporations put limits on people, not because they have to but because they need to. What you are going to make within a few thousand dollars per year is already set in stone before you arrive. I know, I've been there.

Jeepers! There are websites out there that are going to tell you what you are worth before you even apply for a job! The fix is in people! Now look at self-employment, even if it is part time. Ten thousand dollars per year in income equals half a million dollars extra over 50 years! We're only a few pages in and you've made half a million! Maybe I should have charged more for the book?

There is a better way however. Read along and I will free you from the "Golden Handcuffs" that bind the masses to their jobs. You do know what "Golden Handcuffs" are don't you? **The Golden Handcuffs of Corporate America is the**

false sense of security employees have at their jobs. They fell like it's here today and will be tomorrow so why rock the boat? Is that what you want? Is it really what you want? Two weeks a year vacation if you are lucky. Crap medical benefits that you might as well be paying yourself? How about them sick days? And, why don't people use them when they are sick?

Ok mister know it all, what can you possibly have to say that is going to change my life, direction or my financial stability? That is what you are thinking now isn't it? I don't have to be a mind reader to realize someone that has been brainwashed for generations is going to have questions or reservations. Listen up butternuts, I've lived through it already several times. Here is my story.

My own corporate story involves a well-known national retailer in the small to mid-sized footprint realm. I started out as an order taker on the telephone in a spacious four by four cubicle making $7.50 an hour. At that time I would pray for overtime and was basically on a leash except for lunch time. I worked hard (well maybe diligently since it certainly wasn't hard) and soon was promoted to an assistant buyer.

It was now my great pleasure to work in a six foot by six foot cubicle for $25,000 a year. Now that was the life, woo weee! That lasted about a week until I realized I still couldn't afford much. The best part was that I worked for a complete moron! It was my extreme pleasure to jump at his every whim like a puppet on a string! Oh the fun we had, there were his mistakes to fix, and all of his short comings were so evident! I almost forgot the best part! After a few years I maxed out my salary at $28,000, how friggin great is that! Then I got to tell my pregnant wife I was limited for the rest of my career there! Fantastic!

Limits, corporate life seems to be all about limits! When you have to work, when to go home, how much I was ALLOWED TO MAKE, how special is that? It's that special kind of reality that only the SUCKER that has lived through it can appreciate! Is that the life I wanted? Would you sign up for that mission? Oh, some of you have……

Well, the good news was we were bought out by a bigger company and my office was moved to California! Uh, my office was but we weren't. Luckily I was such a good employee that the puppet masters from California decided I was needed as an Assistant Manager at a local retail store! And get this I got a big fat pay cut to stay with the company! That's right my wife was knocked up again and I got to deliver the news! There aint nothing like a completely hormonally enraged woman blubbering at the stove! Life was good.

So, anybody seen a pay cut to keep their job recently??? Come on, I know some of you have! Kind of hard to swallow, like road kill with the fur still on it. Truth is they got you by the nut sack! What are you going to say??? Are you going to tell the bastard no? I didn't think so. Wanna talk about freedom? How about using as many question marks as I want????? You can do it too if you take over your destiny!

I have now decided to single space and then type without using paragraphs for a while. Back to my retail life.

The store was a fun place to work. You see, along with my diminishing mental health status from being someone else's meat puppet for years, the rest of the employees were nuttier than squirrel crap! The best part was the district manager hated my boss! Boy those visits were special! Finally old Norman couldn't take it any longer and tossed his boss the keys. By the sheer fact that nobody else could be talked into the job I was elected Manager by default. The pay raise took me up to just short of what I was making before the pay cut. Guess what? Baby number three was on the way and the hormones were kicking in! I just let the pay increase be a surprise. What was I going to say? Great news babe, I still make less than what I used to! Yup, my wife and I were both having sex, but I was getting up the poop chute! Sound familiar? A few years went by and I was given incremental increases (their terms for cost of living raises) and I was informed I would be making $33,000 per year until the end of time or salaries were adjusted. Great news! I know knew exactly what they were going to value my life at!

Having problems reading without paragraphs? Ok, I'll switch back to a more traditional format. Where was I??? Oh yeah, my life's worth was valued at 33K per year. No matter how many hours and how much money the store made I was LIMITED to a salary set by someone I had never met or talked to. Fan friggin tastic I tell you!

Think my work life sucked? Check out Jim Steiners' story about himself and his father's experiences! Well here we go, you want to work for corporate America? This is a story about my father who spent his whole life working for a paycheck. He was one of the smartest men I ever knew, when I say smart I tell you he is absolutely brilliant!!

He worked 60 hours a week 6 days a week and never took a day off. We had nice clothes, a nice home but I didn't have a father fulltime because he was too busy making someone else rich!! Sure, we spent some time together but it wasn't always quality time. Here is his story in a nut shell. For 40 years he was a hard worker and company man 100% loyal. When he retired he got a $763.00 a month social security income, $202.00 pension, two ulcers, bad cholesterol and a Timex watch!! Come on really!!Not to mention he even got a divorce in the deal!!!

Sounds like Pop's is living out the American Dream, or is it a nightmare. I bet if he knew now what he didn't know then things would be different! How many Americans take that regret to their graves? It won't be this guy!

Welcome to corporate America. Now onto my own story. I wanted to be like my father, but I didn't know if I wanted to work like a dog. I was working for a landscape company in the fall of 1986 when winter came and my boss told me he was gonna lay me off until spring, no pay!! Aint that a bitch! I agreed and moved on.

On January 6,1987 I called an ad in the newspaper it was kinda vague, I mean I needed a seeing eye dog just to get to the interview! With no clue I had no other choice but to check out the job. All that I know it said 400 a week guaranteed and that was good enough for me. After all, I was 19 years old and needed a job. I got interviewed and the fast talking guy told me to call back at 5 and he would have an answer for me. I really didn't think I would get it, but I called back anyway.

This was his response "welcome aboard, you start training tomorrow"! I thought, what in the world was I getting trained for, but I really didn't care. I had landed my first corporate America Job!! Or at least I thought!!

The next day I showed up for training, and there were 30 other people in the room! I started thinking, this must be a huge business. Wrong again, by the end of the training there were only 5 of us, but we were the right 5, so I thought.

Step back one minute. The first day of training this fast talking dude stands in front of the group talking about **money, bonuses and OPPORTUNITY!!** I had no clue what he was talking about. Twenty minutes later some other fast talking dude brings in a vacuum cleaner and gives us a complete demonstration and then says, **I have been with company for 1 year and I am already making over 1,000.00 a week**, I said to myself, no way!!

There was something about all of these people who worked there, **they all had nice cars, great hair, talked like they knew what was up and always flashed 100 dollar bills**. I knew from that day forward, that I was gonna be just like them.

That started my 24 year career in direct sales. In case you were wondering, it was with the Kirby Company, the greatest company I have ever been associated with, because of the structure and training I received was priceless. Absolutely hands down the best training anyone could ever receive, I still use it and train with it today! My seminars are based around Direct Sales that I learned from the Kirby Company to this day.

Back to the story. I learned that the harder I worked the luckier I got. **I made so much money selling dirt suckers door to door as a salesman, that I was able to buy my first house at 20 years of age!! Good bye job, hello opportunity!** I knew from that point in my life, I would never work for anyone ever again and I didn't!! Now there was a lot of stuff in between there in my story, and some of things will be in the book, others are taught in our seminars and trainings. I became a top producer in the direct sales industry as a salesman, manager and then as a factory distributor with the Kirby Co.

It was not a get rich quick deal, it was a process and a program that had to be done right and followed to the tee... My first year as a salesman I made $78,000.00 in 1987. I was 19 and turned 20 in April of that year. I worked my own hours, knocked on any door I wanted and **had time to spend my money on whatever I wanted, and believe me I did just that!!! At 26 years of age I probably made close to a million dollars and at 27 I did!** A Million dollars earned in the direct sales industry!! Who was gonna pay me a million dollars? Me that's who!!!

I knew I was worth more, because I knew how to generate business or income where there wasn't any. I knew I could be dropped out of a helicopter anywhere in the world, and all I needed was a Kirby and a demo kit and I could get rich!! Period. I wasn't an order taker, a sales clerk, didn't count on people to walk in my store. I went out, found customers, did presentations and closed sales. I learned how to close harder than anyone.

I watched tapes, read books, and listened to tapes in my car wherever I went. I was closing all the time and it didn't matter who or what was going on, I was closing. Sales is one of the oldest professions in the world, I think the oldest one is prostitution, but then again something had to be sold there too!!

Can you see how Jim's sales career differed than my job? I was limited in what I could make, while Jim was free to earn as much as he could. He picked a product to stand behind. He got up every morning and made it to work. Was he happier than most knowing that he held his destiny in his own hands? You bet your ass he was!

You see when working for other people, you are always limited, someone else is in control of your destiny, even if your near the top. Talk about pyramid schemes? Corporate America is the biggest pyramid scheme unleashed upon the population in the history of man! You don't need sand and don't even need to be in Egypt to see it! The guy at the top makes all the money right? Take the time to draw out the management of the company you work for some time, its true!

My corporate life went on like this for years. Outgrow one position, and move to a bigger store or company for more money. I look at that time as my prostitution days. I was basically a whore that moved from one place to another for a few dollars.

One day I guess my ass was a little sore and I had enough. I sat there and thought about the tens of millions I had made for other people and decided I needed to make that money for myself. The problem is, how do I do it on my own? There were a few truths that I had to realize, which included I take to heart a few things about the difference between a J.O.B. and a career.

J.O.B. Stands for just over broke. For the vast majority of Americans the harsh reality of working for other people, there is more week at the end of the money than there is money at the end of the week. It's a very true fact unless you are a member of the "lucky sperm club". (Related to upper management) I'm sure if you think hard enough you will come up with a few of these in your life. **I look at a job like being a fish in a tank, you can live, but what is your quality of life?**

When you accept a job you are accepting your destiny. Your fate is sealed, the deal is done and you have sold your soul to the devil. Start looking for strings pal, somebody will be jerking them sooner or later!

My oldest son learned this lesson by his mid-twenties. Being a reasonably intelligent person he realized something wasn't quite right. You see, he has worked for different HVAC companies since he was fifteen years old.

The last company he worked for asked him to find things wrong by let's say not the most moral methods. When he refused to do this, his hours magically dried up! Begrudgingly he started to get with their program, however he started getting anxiety attacks because he knew what they were making him do wasn't Kosher.

To make a long story short, he now owns his own business and is quite successful. To a great extent he now has no anxieties about work. He changed his life by taking his destiny into his own hands! Was it a little scary for him at first? Sure it was. Walk up to him and offer him a job with a company and see how he replies.

In corporate America are you really any more than a number? In a corporation when you accept your position you are assigned a number. This number will stay with you for the entire time you are with them. **Much like a worker bee in a hive, you are now a drone to**

the queen. Your job is the same every day even though you may wear a different tie to think you may be an individual. You sit in a cubicle just like the next person. Like a field of corn you existence there is in your row. Hi, I'm 07731 my cubicle is the third one on the left in row five. Shit you might as well be one of those people in that Matrix movie with the hoses attached! Then when you switch jobs you need to brag or lie about your time at the last corporate teat! Or, how about I am 07731 out of 10482 resistance is futile. You will be assimilated.

Ever wonder why postal workers shoot so many people? We all know the government lacks a certain finesse when operating. Now imagine that same inbred dysfunctional family operating a business? No wonder their employees go postal!

Careers do not require a resume! One of the biggest bullshit things about resumes is the part where you list your former jobs and employers. You might as well be giving them the names of a slaves former owners! Yes sir, I was owned for a while by this one, and then that one had their way with me for 75K a year. What complete crap! Personally show me a resume in good crayon colors and I would be impressed more than a double spaced, starched shorts document that has been spell checked, grammar tested and perfectly punctuated. As a matter of fact, if you said you ate a previous employers brains with a bowl of Fava Beans, would anyone notice? Give them references like the President of the United States or maybe three deceased Senators. Will they catch it? I doubt it.

Corporate America has created this Bovine mentality in its workers. Everybody get in a line, make your resume just like the last persons, and mooooove in a single file line to get a ring in your nose. Now you can be lead to your stall (cubicle) and we can milk you for all you have! There you sit, day after day month after month in captivity while you digest crap that is pitchforked to you.

Most employees are given the "Mushroom Treatment" especially when it comes to their future. You're like a calf being led to slaughter one day when your job is gone and nobody saw it coming!

Careers rely on you! Put on your big boy pants for this one! If you are going to take on life yourself, you have to be able to rely on yourself! This is the point where most people piss their pants and say never mind. The simple fact is that it is easier suck on some other teat than have to make money on your own money. The fact that we as a people are so afraid to detach is darned frightening.

Yes, the corporate teat will feed you every week as long as you are valuable to them, but wouldn't it be cool if you were valuable to yourself? Even if it started out slow?

Nobody with any trace of brain matter would tell somebody to just jump in on the deep end. Not even a nut like me who has been at it a while. I can tell you this though. If I can do it you can too!

Successful people do what the unsuccessful are not willing to do. People ask to go picking with me, yet few actually go when I tell them I will pick them up at four in the morning. I just don't get up that early they tell me. How tough is that one? Can't get up to make a two thousand dollar score?? Sure you may come up empty on a particular day, but more often than not it's worth it.

How many times have I told somebody that if they dropped me off at a flea market with $100.00 I could turn it into $500.00 in a week? A bunch, and it's the truth. Who is willing to do it though? Not that many!

I've sat at an auction waiting for hours to bid on a lid that I saw on a pot. I bought that "lid" for five dollars that night. It turned out to be a Chinese shield. Nobody else took a shot on it… They just didn't know. They weren't willing to learn their business!

Jim spent years knocking on doors in his business. After that, he knocked on doors to get others into houses. Are you willing to do that to succeed?

Can you wake up when you need to? Will you work until the job is done? Can you commit to your own success?

At this point if you still don't get it, tear the book up, light it on fire, or use it to level the table. You just aint getting it! If you're a little curious read on…..

This is what I was taught as a kid. Go to school, get good grades and then a job at a company that you can stay at long term. Long term because there would be retirement benefits like a pension when I would retire. If I was lucky I would get a gold watch and retirement dinner too. Let's look at reality. Going to school and getting good grades is important, like really important especially if you need to read and count to any number past twenty. The rest of my sentence is condensed crap.

Things have changed. Will Social Security even exist? Retire on what? Most people make enough to live paycheck to paycheck at best! Do you really want that as your future? Dude, I'm just trying to help you here!

As an employee, what does a company owe you? Fair pay? Forty hours a week? Weekends off? Benefits? How about **None of the above!** What? You got it! Hours are cut back, take it up the shorts! Fair pay, who decides that? Think you have any chance of negotiation? Pension……..nearly pissed myself laughing at that thought! Aside from your cubicle neighbor your departure won't matter. What is todays saying in the workplace? No one is unreplaceable. Yup, just the guy you want jerking your chain for the next five years if you make it that long.

Let's take a look at what I and a lot of people call a career and the rewards. The first principal of a career is that **a career pays you based on your performance!** To a great extent, you decide based on your business choice what you will make. In other words **there are no limits what you can accomplish or what you make!** Chosen properly a career will furnish you the ability to have equity when you are done working. That means **you will have assets to liquidate or have residual income from your business when you are done!** If the business you want to go into won't do this then it doesn't make sense and it surely won't make many dollars! More on that later.

Before some of you think I'm some kind of screwball that wants you to tell your boss to kiss your ass and quit tomorrow, you haven't heard the rest of the plan yet. Most people have at least some down time they can make use of nearly every day. **This opens nearly everybody to work on their job full time and their fortune part time.**

This thought is beyond the average person and may not seem to make sense at first, but **there are many ways to make money that can exceed your jobs salary in time.** Many times I have been told I am very lucky to earn a living the way I do. When I tell them I can show them how, most just have a blank stare and are silent. The thought of being self-sufficient is too much of a chance for them. After all knowing that you are Mr. Turdpopper's favorite target on a Monday morning does have its charm. Kind of like a yeast infection. But hey, if you like a double yeast infection more power to you!

Seriously though, how hard is it to do my thing? I'm not the sharpest knife in the drawer so there is hope for you too. For instance **I know people that routinely make 100K on EBay.** That's right with some effort a person can make decent money working a few days a week or a good living (if 100k is considered good). Personally I have done up to 70K per year buying and selling things that people had no idea of the value. This was putting in a total of about twenty five hours per week picking at Flea Markets, Auctions and Estate Sales. Hey, the dead people aren't going to take it with them!

Take these cases as examples of what a person can do. I have two friends that I affectionately look to as uncles. Pauli and BooBoo have different backgrounds yet remarkably similar outcomes.

Pauli was an auto mechanic that went to flea markets and such on weekends, while BooBoo was a school teacher who had the same weekend past time. **Pauli got tired of turning a wrench when his part time income exceeded what he made full time.** Pauli leads a life off the grid, using what he has picked as a bank account. When he wants a few thousand dollars to spend, he goes into his vault and liquidates a few possessions **for cash, no checks accepted!** If I had to guess at his net worth it would be well over a million dollars. **One day I was going on a private pick and he asked me how much** money I had on me. When I told him I had about fifteen hundred in my pocket, he reached into his pocket and handed me another five grand just in case. Name a corporate guy that can do that on any particular day!

BooBoo always gave his earnings from his teaching job to his wives, and trust me he has had a bunch of them. **His secret to having money was his part time business.** BooBoo picked and collected for over thirty years and has **paid for all of his divorces in cash! Today he relies on his collection to fund his retirement!**

There are many BooBoos and Paulies out there. They lead a happy life and pretty much have what they want. Heck BooBoo takes off to Florida at the first hint of frost!

Trash picking can be very lucrative. I have several contacts that drive through rich neighborhoods at night before the trash is picked up. The stuff they find is amazing to say the least! Most of them make 75K plus a year. So much for trash pickers being losers.

Have I always been successful? The answer is no! My worm farming business went bust because I didn't realize that spring water (bottled) can have chlorine in it. So I wound up sending several thousand Canadian Night Crawlers to their own personal hell.

I even owned a commercial fishing business for several years and went out when fuel prices spiked and lobster prices dipped. So yes, I've experienced some setbacks.

These are examples of businesses, but by no means are they your only options! Can you do mechanical work? Fix lawnmowers? Fill your truck with scrap? Buy a hot dog cart? Ways to make money are almost limitless! All but opening up a three hundred by three hundred clearing behind Uncle Leo's house to grow Hemp can be long lasting and to some point lucrative businesses.

Another although misunderstood option is **Network Marketing**. I knew it you say! He's off his rocker you say! It's a scam you say! I have to admit that Network Marketing is not for everybody, but it could be for a lot of people if they just understood the truth. Network marketing is one of the oldest professions out there. After all without a Network, how did Mr. and Mrs. Medieval let people know about their saber tooth tiger rug business? How did Fred Flintstone find his bowling league? How did you know the Blacksmith's address when your horse had a flat?

Listen up, this has a big up side to it. Sure there were scams out there, but a majority of these companies make people a lot of money!

How do Network Marketing companies make people money? The long and short of it goes something like this. To have a business you need something to make, do a service or sell. Ok, you say? No argument there. Well, these people have already thought out the project, developed the product, and have it ready for the market.

What makes Network Marketing Companies different is that they use a different way to sell and distribute their products. That's really it in a nutshell folks. They can offer a quality product at affordable prices because of the lack of cost of hourly employees. Many of them have and need a large headquarters or warehouse facility to run their businesses.

Hey man, these dudes are Corporations! You're getting boned a different way! Sorry to disappoint you Slick, but the way they market makes them much different from the traditional corporate giant. You can make as much or as little as you like. You go where you want and sell when you want. You get freedom and opportunity at the same time. Want to take off on Wednesday to go fishing? It's up to you! Soccer practice at six? No problem. See the difference?

Who is a Network Marketer? Anybody that makes part or a majority of their income from meeting people. Here are a few examples:

If you make money by

Selling Insurance

Selling Real Estate

Selling Stocks or Bonds

Selling Cars, Trucks, Motorcycles or Boats

Selling just about anything else

You are a Network Marketer already!

Here's a quick question for you. Are you "that guy"? The one who knows everybody. The person that people always ask if you know someone who does this or that? If you are, you should probably consider it.

Here's a quick fact for you. **A person is much more likely to become a millionaire by Network Marketing than by most other professions!** In fact your odds of making a decent living of say 100K or better are five times better than at a job. Aren't they all "pyramid schemes"? I hear a lot about "pyramids and "earn and burn". Is this all true? It must be a scam if you don't work for somebody? Is it even legal?

What is a "Pyramid Scheme"? Well, if some guy is trying to sign you up in Egypt it's probably a pyramid. Pyramid schemes are illegal. They offer no tangible product or benefits. Money is made purely by signing up people.

But, when I draw out the pay plan it looks like a pyramid shape. What's up with that? Draw the corporate structure of any company, they all look like pyramids. My company is an upside down pizza slice.

Ask yourself a question when thinking about a Network Marketing business. Is there a product that can be seen and delivered? If there is, then it is most probably a legal business. Some of these companies that use Network Marketing or Direct Sales can be quite large!

Can I get rich quick? The two best ways I know of to get rich quick are the lottery or killing off a relative that has you in their will. I recommend neither of them as a profession even if it's only part time. **Direct Sales and network Marketing build wealth much like a brick layer putting up a wall. Each row or layer gets them closer to the top.** In time you can build something quite impressive.

For instance, the king of direct sales Berkshire Hathaway, Warren Buffet's company uses direct Sales (door to door etc.) to market their Kirby vacuum cleaners. Now, if that's not a well-known company then I don't know what is! Now I don't even come close to telling you to go door to door in your business, but if a Girl Scout can do it……..

If you think I'm recommending something I am not ready to do guess again. Jim and I have done quite well in the past as a team running a distributorship. You see, I worked for Kirby and trained people to sell and overcome objections with Jim.

Here is the most misunderstood thing about Network Marketing. **It's called Network Marketing for a reason! It's not Netsitonyourbuttmarketing, Nettakeanapmarketing, Netdonothingandgetpaidfotitmarketing, it is indeed honest work!** The number one reason most people fail is because they have no idea what they are supposed to do! They know they need to find people but lack the skills needed to succeed.

The business I am now involved with sells extended warranties directly to consumers. These products are insured by Lloyds of London and include Home Electronics, Autos and even complete Home Warranty products. This company supplies a very high quality website www.mywarrantyrewards.com/stevehorvath which has a back room that keeps up with my sales and agents.

This company provides pay for each agent I sign and an override for agents they bring on and so on. Not only that, but I receive residual income every month for each policy as they renew. Remember what I said about retirement and continual pay (residuals)? The best part is that the more people I sign up, the higher my residual percentage. The most important thing about these businesses is they require little up-front investment and can be done at your pace. There is no need to detach from the teat until you are ready to. How do I achieve success beyond my friends in this business?

The first thing you need to realize in any business venture is that even your best friends may not support your decision. There will always be those who want you to fail and will be waiting to tell you so. The best course for this is to not push things on them. In fact, the most successful people I meet in the industry aren't pushy at all. As a matter of fact they use a very basic way of communicating with people to create interest.

So, what about this "earn and burn" thing I hear about? Earn and burn is an industry term used for people who really aren't interested in putting forth an honest effort. They make pitches to family and friends, make a few dollars and fizzle out. **In many cases this is due to a lack of training and support by those that got them involved!** The group we run has regular meetings where we re enforce the basics and **coach those that are deserving.**

Who deserves help and who doesn't? For our operation the answer is simple. Show up to our weekly meetings and put forth any kind of effort. **I would rather have one green agent**

with some kind of motivation than a room full of lazy experienced people. You know what people say. When you're green you're growing and when you're ripe you're rotting! Have an open mind people! Learn from others and repeat the process.

Here is what I recommend to our group:

Have the "all the time attitude".

Own business cards.

Engage people in conversation every day.

When people are interested use a 3 way call.

Support the people you sponsor.

Have realistic goals.

With these six ingredients it is totally realistic to be a millionaire in five years or less. Five to ten thousand a month is extremely doable in this same time period for under achievers. Do you make that now in forty hours a week? Do you want to? Let's look at the list of ingredients.

Have the "all the time attitude". People are glued to this thing called full time and part time. It's like their afraid of being tazered if they step out of bounds. Did you start out part time people will ask me? My answer makes them think I obsess about everything. Hey don't taze me man! I tell them I am working all the time. This simply means that I am always open to the possibility of meeting or talking with someone who doesn't know about what I have to offer.

Most people have their shorts so starched that they can't even imagine being capable of doing two projects at the same time. For Christ's sake people wake up and smell the coffee! Let's say your cubicle neighbor sees that you seem to be happier than normal because of your new enterprise. What are you going to do? You have two choices, shut up and hope Mrs. Hangnail doesn't hear you two talking or just mention you have something good going on the side. Think fast Skippy, which one is it going to be?

Your neighbor is going to react in one of two ways. He's going to hate you and how God has cursed his life, or be curious about what you have going on. A seed has been planted.

Own Business Cards. Really? I mean really? How easy is this one? This one goes right by most people and I wonder why. Business cards can be a great tool or waste of money depending on how they are used. **But you need to have them to use them!**

With a little imagination a card can actually be interesting enough for a person to be more curious about who you are and what you do. Too many people are boxed into this same rubber stamp format that every one of the most boring cards has. Of course the cards should have your contact info on it but, then what? There is usually an option to put a title right below your name. **Your title alone can be what**

interests a person in you. Think about it for a second, you're Joe Blow and what is it you do? Damnit! Think! Use your imagination for once! How about **Joe Blow Life Changer or even Builder of Wealth? There are so many options out there!** Any way you look at it your business card can be a great tool. Later we will show you how to use it.

Engage people in conversation every day. Dude, how easy is that? How can you network without talking to anybody? I'm not talking about trying to sell something to everyone you meet! Say more than one word to the person you buy your morning coffee from. Greet them with something simple. Good morning Bob, how is the coffee today? Eventually people will ask questions about yourself. At worst they will tell you which one they urinated in because they hate their job.

Have you ever heard of the **Yeager Principal?** There was a man named Yeager who wanted to be a successful sales person. Every day he would start the day with ten pennies in his right pocket. As he would have conversation with people he would move a penny to his left pocket. Yeager refused to go home until all of his pennies were in his left pocket. As it turns out he is now a retired millionaire, just from meeting people. Think about how many people you talk to a day now. The total is probably the same six or seven not counting your wife, kids, shrink or prostitutes. Yeager talked to 50 people in a week or 2,600 people per year. That's networking!

Who is a customer? How do I qualify them? How do I stop from prejudging people? One topic that I see being a problem in our industry is that a lot of people tend to prejudge the customer or the person we are trying to recruit. I have been in customers' homes that really had no need for what I was selling. She probably should bought another item that they needed more, but because of the desire to want what I had they decided to buy. People buy what they want, not what the need. Nobody needs a Lear Jet, but people buy them. Nobody needs a football team, but people buy them.

I am gonna give you an example of this based on a personal story. I was fairly new in my selling career and I was in a woman's house in Trenton, NJ putting on a presentation. You have to realize this isn't the richest neighborhood in the area. When I walked up to the porch, I noticed that there were no steps. The top two were rotted out so I had to jump on the porch with my stuff just to get in the house! There was a stack of newspapers as high as the porch ceiling and they were so old they had turned three different colors. The old refrigerator on the porch and washing machine as well were pretty rotted out, you get the picture??

Remember before when I told you it wasn't the greatest neighborhood? In hindsight I probably should have had half a dozen armed guards, three attack dogs and a full S.W.A.T. team standing by.

As I entered the house I heard a voice say to me "I am in here baby, bring what you got and show me in here". I was scared, I couldn't find where "in here was", so I followed her voice and there she was. It was about 100 degrees in this house and I was afraid to even ask for a glass of water, but I did. That was always a good ice breaker for me, it showed that I trusted them and the trusted me. Well, there she was, Ms. Johnson sitting there with a fan in her hand trying to keep herself cool. She said, "Show me what you got sonny", so I did what she told me. I forgot to mention that I was selling vacuum cleaners and she didn't have a stitch of carpet in the whole house. I am thinking there is no way this woman needs a vacuum, I think she needs a bulldozer instead.

She watched my half ass presentation, because I was prejudging her all the way to the end and really wasn't into it. When I finished she asked me how much it was. I had no intentions of even telling her the price, I just wanted to get out of that house and move on to a qualified buyer!! Besides,, I had already lost about 5lbs during my presentation and almost had a heat stroke. So I took out my closing pad and wrote down the price and set it on the table. Normally I would be very aggressive and sit down next to the customer and show them the options they had and try to find out how they needed to be sold!!

Well, her response was" would you do better if I bought two"? I really didn't know what to say, so I said what every great salesperson would say "how much better do you want me to do"? **Now at this point I really knew I had a sale, but here goes my prejudging practices that I learned from the old negative guys at the**

office, the ones who are starving and couldn't close a door, if they had to.

There was no way her credit was gonna go through in my mind! So, I asked her this. "How would you like to pay for these two machines"? Her answer floored me and this was it "well, I have another home in Florida that I go to in the winter and I could use one there too". Then she continued, and I WANT one here as well. So I will buy both of them from you today, if you're willing to ship one to Florida." Ok, I said how do you want to pay?? Here is what she did next, again it blew my mind. She reached into her Bra, that's right, her Bra and she pulled out $2,400.00 in cold hard cash and said to me "would you count this for me baby, I don't have my glasses on me"?

What the heck just happened!! To this day I don't know whether it was a question or a statement. She bought two machines from me, that's what just happened! **Never ever prejudge anyone for any reason what so ever!!!**

More words of wisdom on Prejudging. We also tend to pre judge agents. Okay since we are on the prejudging subject, I want to tell you it's even more important not to prejudge or become prejudice towards anyone that you are recruiting or trying to bring them into your business.

I can guarantee you one thing, and that is, you haven't recruited or hired your best person in your business yet and he or she is still out there waiting for opportunity to fall in the lap.

This reminds me a story, again from my own personal file in direct sales. One of my better skills was the ability to recruit and train good people in the sales game. One Monday I ran an ad for my business in a local newspaper and about 25 people showed up. I interviewed them and nobody stuck out as anything but a warm body. It was a long day and I was super tired and needed a break. I locked the office door and was packing up for the day when I heard someone banging on the outside door.

I got up and answered it. This kid was standing in my doorway with curly long red hair, freckles and an all-around ragged look. He was wearing shorts, a tank top and had six tattoos that visible to me because of his outfit.

 He also wore a pair of beat up vans and water bottle in his hand and he was sweating profusely. I said to him "are you lost"? He laughed at me and said "No, I am here for the job interview." Now you have to understand he looked just like Opie from Mayberry, but there was something about him. So I responded to him "do you have a car"? He started laughing at me again and said "no, I took the bus and then rode my skateboard the rest of the way sir and I am truly sorry for being late".

I mean, what are you gonna say to him!! So, I told him to come in and fill out an application. This kid had more talent in his little finger, than most people have in their whole body!! He was a quick learner, hard worker and a great closer! I was able to train him the way all people should be trained. Out of the 25 people that showed up the next day, he was one of two who actually stuck it out and decided that he was going to make a living like me, in direct sales. He was a top producer year after year, month after month. All I had to do was keep his head in the game and keep him motivated.

Believe me that was a lot of work, but it paid off. He was such a big asset to my organization that I wish I had 10 of him, but I think they broke the mold on that one!! He eventually became promoted and went on to have a great career in direct sales. Opie made me and my business so much money, I didn't even want to promote him, but he earned it and I gave back what was given to me at around the same age as he was. That red head was truly a diamond in the rough.

Now you have to understand I searched through piles of coal, just to find that one diamond. Guess what? I almost missed it. If I would have went with my instincts I would have prejudged him all the way to the curb, put him back on that bus and he would of had to ride his skateboard to another interview. Thank god I didn't. **Direct Sales or Network Marketing are two of the greatest business models in America, and I tell you this, do not prejudge anyone, and I mean anyone!** If they have no money, tell them you been looking for them for years. Give them a chance, after all, if you're reading this book, someone gave you a chance!!!

When people show interest put them on a three way call. This is a powerful tool that we use in our team. How this goes is we bring in someone with more experience in the business than we have. **Unless you are already the man, there is no problem bringing in an expert.**

You can sit back and be a more or less neutral party while the prospect talks with someone of "authority".

Support the people you sponsor! Man, you won't believe how important this one is! How many people have tried direct sales or Network Marketing and failed because of the lack of this! Here go sell this, you'll do great! Practice on your family and friends! Next thing you know the poor bastard is out of friends and out of luck! **Real legitimate businesses want to grow and thrive!** People are like animals. The more treats they receive, the more they will perform. This is why we do our three way calls and coach those who show effort!

Why such a starched or canned presentation you ask? Aren't I with the freedom to my own destiny? This is the way we do it because it works. I myself have side stepped the process and my own closing rate went down. Our team is free to work as they want, however the team chooses to stick with this process because they know it works.

Have realistic goals. Without a goal, what can you possibly accomplish? How do you know when you've made it? Goals need to be realistic and attainable.

If goals are set too high, then all you will accomplish is failure. We recommend that our people set a goal of selling one person. The next goal is three total. After that flurry, recruiting 2 people per month may be all a person can accomplish, but it all depends on that person.

Let's do some quick math. You can get started today with signing up 3 people in your 30 days. In our business that would give you a bonus plus an increase of your override percentage. In the next 11 months you recruit one person per month. At the end of 12 months you would have 14 people you would be getting an override of 25% of what they make. Not bad, you now have 14 employees! Better than your job? Hell yes! Then recruit one per month and at the end of the 48 months you have 51 people paying YOU!!! How great is that?????? Did I mention the residuals from all of the warranties that are sold???? Guess what?

You are probably moving to a new neighborhood or buying your own island! Is it realistic? YES! Is it doable? YES! Does it take effort? YES! Is it a real business? YES! YES! YES! Have people made Millions in the Network Marketing business? YES, thousands of them have!

This is how I did it. Jim Steiner came to me one day with information on the warranty company. Knowing him from an early age and his background if felt like it had some promise. **Then I did my own research!** I found videos, commentaries, reviewed their products etc.

Remember that **I knew ahead of time this was a Direct Sales Network Marketing Company.** After a few days I called Jim back and said, "Sign me up"!

From there I made a list of everyone I knew. I mean everybody! Later, I deleted a few deceased and terminally ill people to get my final list. List in hand I made contact with each person.

Since this was a new business in the area, Jim and I had decided to hold an introductory meeting for our friends and family. We had twelve total people in attendance and all twelve signed up that night! One hundred percent conversion was a shock to both of us! Both of my sons who own their own business signed up as well as my neighbor who just came for the food! **They came to me and asked to become part of our team!** Here's what the meeting amounted to. We showed a ten minute and twenty seven second intro video and had the person that recruited Jim speak about his experience with the company. **There was no hard sell or get rich quick talk.** Just the simple truth was all that was needed.

Since then we have hosted a team meeting every week. In those meetings we talk about our successes and challenges. After all, **we support the people we sponsor, don't we?**

What are our actual team meetings about? We coach people on how to approach the subject of our business. Our approach is really simple. First we need to know from previous conversation whether they are looking to change jobs, make extra money or even indifferent to the whole thing. In our business there are three types of people. Those that always buy warranties, sometimes buy warranties and never buy warranties.

Hey, that's a great approach! We ask them to identify themselves and qualify them as a customer! It goes something like this:

Can I ask you a question? When it comes to extended warranties do you get them all the

time, sometimes, or never? Bam! The ice has been broken in the conversation! Not only this, but you have a clue as to how to proceed! If they say always sign them up! Slam bam thank you ma'am sign here buddy! Ok you sold one or more warranties, but what's next?

Next comes an important question. If you like what you just purchased will you tell your friends? Will you have them get in touch with me? (Here's a spot for business cards or even to get referrals) Then ask if they would rather make the money signing them up or if I can make the money. **Oh, you would like to make a few extra dollars? Let me show you how……**

At this point we can show them the video we have and even call someone more experienced to answer questions. This way we recruit agents and sell warranties at the same time. **It really isn't rocket science…..**

How about the person that says sometimes? How do we crack that rock? We ask questions! What do you buy warranties for? What if I could warranty just about anything electronic in your house for a dollar per day? How about offering a free month trial? If they show any kind of interest we can move forward, if not talk about the weather or change the conversation. Now may not be the best time.

What happens if they agree with everything but still won't buy? Ask them why. What is it that's keeping you from buying? Do you not see the value? Is it my breath? Then clam up! Shut your mouth and listen. You are about to get the real reason. If you can overcome this objection you are home free! Sign them up!

Now, you need to realize that people that never buy warranties can be hard to convert. These people usually have had bad experiences or just aren't informed about what the world holds.

The best way to find out why is to ask? **Really, why not? Have you had a bad experience with them?** Trust me, you are about to find out why or they are just ignorant. If you can engage them about it you're in the game! If not maybe find a new game.

Then there are the people that you have been being nice to and speaking with when you get coffee or any other place you frequent. They are bound to ask you what you do. They may even tell you they aren't happy where they are. Trust me it's going to happen sooner or later.

"Hey Fred, I never asked what you do?",said the cashier at the local shop. Ok you're up! Uh, I sell stuff......NO WRONG ANSWER!!! I have my own business, a friend got me into it and it's really great! Much better butternuts! Here check out the video on my website. You're getting it now! Hey, how about I call you after you've watched it and then we can talk about it? DING, DING,

DING, WINNER! That's the way to do it! Even better you can call them and have them watch the video while you are getting a three way call going! This is the easiest way to close a sale and recruit an agent.

The next person you will may run into is called "The Superstar". I call them Superstars because they have great qualities. They smile and greet you where they work. They are always cheery and usually have tons of friends. Landing a Superstar or at least who you think is a Superstar can be quite a boon to your business. One word of caution about a Superstar: **Superstars rarely live up to your expectation of them.** They may be too social or too laid back to give full effort to the cause. I would much rather have hungry average people than a lazy Superstar. In fact chasing these human unicorns can really distract you. If you do capture one, it'll be well worth it!

Among the stew of humanity you will also find the "Festering Wounded". **The Festering Wounded are people who have had bad experiences with Multi-Level Marketing, Direct Sales and Network Marketing.** In fact some of these may have been infected by exposure to real Pyramid and Ponzi Schemes.

You can tell you're around the Festering Wounded by the way they twitch and ooze puss from their wounds around words like up line, opportunity and recruit. A few have been known to fall into cardiac arrest at the mention of a "power leg". Yes, they are a sad sort, but some of them can be saved. In this case you need to listen to their story until blood literally runs out of your ears before re assuring them about your business. Tell them about the great support available and how you will personally help them succeed.

My favorite is the **Network Marketing Groupie. This is an easy sell because they really want to succeed!** They do carry some baggage though. Usually they have been in several companies but haven't really done anything. They can make the meetings and recite what you say verbatim, but they just seem to go nowhere. There is hope for them though. Training, coaching and taking small steps can be the key.

While I try not to pre judge people there is a group called **"The Scammers"**.

Scammers are called that because anything that doesn't come from the government is a scam, at least in their eyes it is. Hey Marty, I'm getting involved in a new project. Want to hear about it? **It's a scam.** I'm making money already. **Scam.** I made $6,000.00 last week. **It's still a scam.** Hey, you know what's not a scam? No Marty what is it? It's the big warm hug I feel when I get my welfare check. Ok Marty, see you later. Don't waste your time with them. If they had the IQ of a tomato plant they would probably listen.

The person you really want to bring in is called **"The Hungry Man"**. **The Hungry Man is characterized by their willingness to listen and follow the steps to success that you instill in them.** They may not be the brightest of the bunch, but they are the bread and butter of the Network Marketing or Direct Sales industry. Often times these are also the most successful.

Now that you can strike up a conversation with just about anyone, you are about out of people aren't you. This is the crossroads of your career and the place where you either make it big or not.

Always remember two things about this business. **To keep growing, you must be able to motivate the team you have to keep them**

growing while recruiting others constantly! Meetings, communications and even contests keep up morale, while the lack of meetings and a lack of communication are like a cancer. Go to meetings often and celebrate the positive. A little babysitting goes a long way in our business!

You are now left with a dilemma, how do I reach people I don't have the ability to now? Well Skippy, what are you going to do? Hire a hot air balloon?

Tattoo your website www.mywarrantyrewards.com/stevehorvath on your forehead? Maybe have a T Shirt made up? How about this, Social Media and free advertising. That's right for about zero dollars you can reach out all over the world, at least to the next county anyhow. Start with Facebook for instance.

Great, I'll bomb Facebook with ads and stuff! Start copying and pasting, right? Slow down sport it just doesn't go like that. My posts are about 90 percent positive thinking, attitude and lifestyle. Why? Because I want people to know me. See the life I lead. Think of me as a positive influence. A few times each week I am approached by people asking questions about what I do or how I make my money. This is how I make first contact with a lot of folks. The truth is Facebook is a great tool, but you cannot build a business solely on this one platform. **Beware of people who tell you otherwise!** Can you recruit a few people? Yes! Can you build a whole business there? NO!

I also get offers to join other businesses, MLM's, Networks etc. The worst part is how terrible most people's approach is. Hey, you need to join my team because I drive a Mercedes was one I recall vividly. Really? I mean really? Why on earth would you think your Mercedes would impress me? I drive a Ford F-350 pickup. Why? Because it fits my lifestyle. Period, end of sentence. I'm sure Mercedes builds a great vehicle, but assuming I would envy what he had was a terrible mistake.

One of the better approaches was, how would you like a free electric bill? It makes a person think. Free electric, let me find out more. It really is a great pitch from a company that has made many millionaires already. It is so good that at the time I offered the person the option of teaming up with me in both businesses. Why they declined I don't know, but too bad for them.

Back to Facebook. Pictures with inspirational captions garner a lot of attention as do short sentences about the promise of the new day and things like that. At this point I am getting three to five new friends per day which is a larger audience for free.

Things to avoid however are porn, racial slurs, and other things which will offend large parts of the audience. Stupid people videos of the population hurting themselves is always good! Bring on the pain! I prefer the genital wrenching skateboard videos. Boy, that's gotta hurt!

The next great freebie available is Craigslist. That's right, the great bazaar of strangeness that is Craigslist can be a great source of people needing money. We offer free marketing seminars all the time and the ad is free! You may wind up with a strange cast of characters ranging from nearly normal to mutant, but hey mutants need to make money too!

Craigslist can also be a great spot to run a help wanted ad. True you're going to spend about twenty five bucks, but you will get five to ten prospects per ad. Here's a sample:

National Warranty Company expanding!

We are looking for experienced Agents!

Check out our video (give website)

Commissions

Bonuses

Overrides

Residuals

Training

Full Time or Part Time

For more info Contact Steve Horvath

Let's look at how this ad is designed. The first line tells you this is a large company. Remember a huge amount of people think bigger is better and somehow has more credibility.

We're a national company who is expanding which implies we are doing well!

Who are we looking for? That's right agents, and experienced ones at that. What does an agent do? Well insurance agents and real estate agents sell stuff. They must be looking for sales people.

They have a website. Great I can research them! Let me search the website out. Hey, they sell extended warranties for just about everything! There are videos too. Wow, they look pretty good.

I wonder how the pay structure is. Hmm it says Commissions, Bonuses, Overrides and Residuals. Seems like I can make money several ways.

Wow, they will even train me. Sounds good so far. I can work full or part time also.

What would it hurt to tell them I am interested? I'll send them my resume....

Meanwhile back at the ranch Steve or Jim gets an email. Hi, this is Mary Butterface and I am looking for meaningful employment in your industry blah, blah, blah, blah…….blah

Mary receives an email from one of us. Hi Mary this is Jim, I am very busy right now but I would like to give you a call tomorrow. What time would be best to contact you? At this time Mary has set her own appointment. If she lives close we can meet at a public place like a coffee shop. If not it's on the phone. For a three way call. Remember to let her know that there are three of you on the line.

In this case we are going to meet at a coffee shop which more times than not it's actually a better circumstance for us.

The next day at two o'clock Jim meets Mary at the coffee shop. He offers to buy her a coffee and they sit down together. The conversation starts off about the weather and how good the coffee is and maybe what their favorite donuts are.

Jim asks Mary if she has any prior sales experience and she says yes and things are going OK so far. Jim then asks Mary if she has checked out the website. Yes, but I'm not sure about a few things is her reply. You know what Mary? I want to call the person who started me out if you don't mind is Jim's response. No problem is her reply. Jim calls another management person to help with the call.

The "expert" fields the questions. What does this do? Well, for starters Jim isn't selling her anything so she continues to trust Jim and the expert. It goes either of two ways from here, she's in or she's out.

In our business there are only two really proven ways to get results with any regularity. They are the face to face which we have just seen and bringing the person to a meeting. I actually prefer the meeting.

Our meetings are the same time and day every week to avoid confusion. There is also food and refreshments like water, coffee and soda. **More than one person has come for the food and signed up.**

Bringing prospects to meetings has many advantages. The prospect can feel the positive energy. They hear success stories and see first-hand that we are available at almost any time to help our agents. When we talk about the warranty company, it's not at them and there is no pressure. As a matter of fact, other than the recognition of being a new attendant at the meeting we don't even talk to them. We do our thing and they listen to it.

At the end, we ask them what they think, not if they are ready to sign up. Sometimes it takes a second call or even a second meeting for people to decide. Our closing rate at meetings is about sixty percent which I feel is pretty darn good.

The care and handling of agents is very important after the sign up. The job has just started at this point for the folks running the show. A sign up and the payoff for it is OK, but the idea is for the agents to be productive for both you and them. The first step is to get their cell number and email, heck friend them on Facebook too. **Constant and free flowing communication is important at this point and beyond.** Include them in group texts and emails recognizing them and their peers' successes. This way they can not only contact you, but other members of the team also.

What other communications do we have with our team? We remind them of meetings, ask our team who is bringing guests, and even if they are bringing snacks.

Will some people fall by the wayside? The answer is yes to be brutally honest. Not every sperm makes it to the egg do they? The people who don't make it lack something. I don't know if it's laziness, lack of motivation or fear. What culminates in these people is ultimately the same. They just don't work. Their efforts fall way short of successful people no matter how you try to help. We can help them polish their rap, but you can't polish a turd.

OK, I'm ready to try this, how do I get started? If you aren't interested in joining my team, make sure the program has some type of credibility. Check them out. Find out how long they have been around. **Longer is not necessarily better in this case.** Companies that have been around for a long time can be too well known. The market for their products can get flooded or there can be competitors on every corner. Cosmetics, Jewelry, Food, Vitamins, and health products have been beaten to death. That's why I chose an extended warranty company. It's relatively new to the Network Marketing category, but customers have already heard of them through retailers.

Look at the payment structure. What is it going to take to earn money? Is it attainable? How often do I get paid? Do I have to make a certain amount to get paid?

What is the cost of getting in? Let's face it, a hundred bucks isn't going to kill most of us as a onetime investment. How about two hundred? Five Hundred? Two thousand? It can get quite pricey out there. Think about what it costs to open a garage, coffee shop or other business. There is a big upside to these programs for a small investment.

How can you live with yourself being a Network Marketer? How do you sleep at night? I sleep very well thank you. This career helps me help people and feel better about myself. Every time I see a person receive a check for one hundred, five hundred or one thousand a month for their efforts and a minimal investment I know I've helped someone get closer to their goals.

Can I do it? We have talked about several paths for a reason. People are not one size fits all. If you have determination, commitment and a desire to succeed then yes this type of life may be for you. **Unlike a corporation, I will not pass judgment on you or tell you what you deserve.**

www.ingramcontent.com/pod-product-compliance
Lightning Source LLC
Chambersburg PA
CBHW071756170526
45167CB00003B/1056